WORLD FOCUS
India
AMANDA BARKER

Contents

Note to the Reader
Some words in this book are printed in **bold** type.
This shows that the word is listed in the glossary
on page 30. The glossary gives a brief
explanation of words that may be new to you.

6773352

Introduction

Tropic of Cancer

Equator

Tropic of Capricorn

India is a large country in Asia, with a complex history and culture. The British ruled most of India from 1849 until 1947. **Mahatma Gandhi** led a non-violent movement towards independence, and in 1947 India became a free country again. India is now the largest **democracy** in the world.

△ **Where is India?**

If you were to travel through India from north to south, you would see many changes in the landscape. The highest mountains are in the north. They are part of the Himalayan mountain range. But right next to them, south of the Himalayas, is the flattest and most fertile land in India. Crops grow very well there. The Ganges River winds its way eastwards towards the Bay of Bengal. To the west is the Thar Desert.

◁ Few plants grow on the dry sands of the Thar Desert.

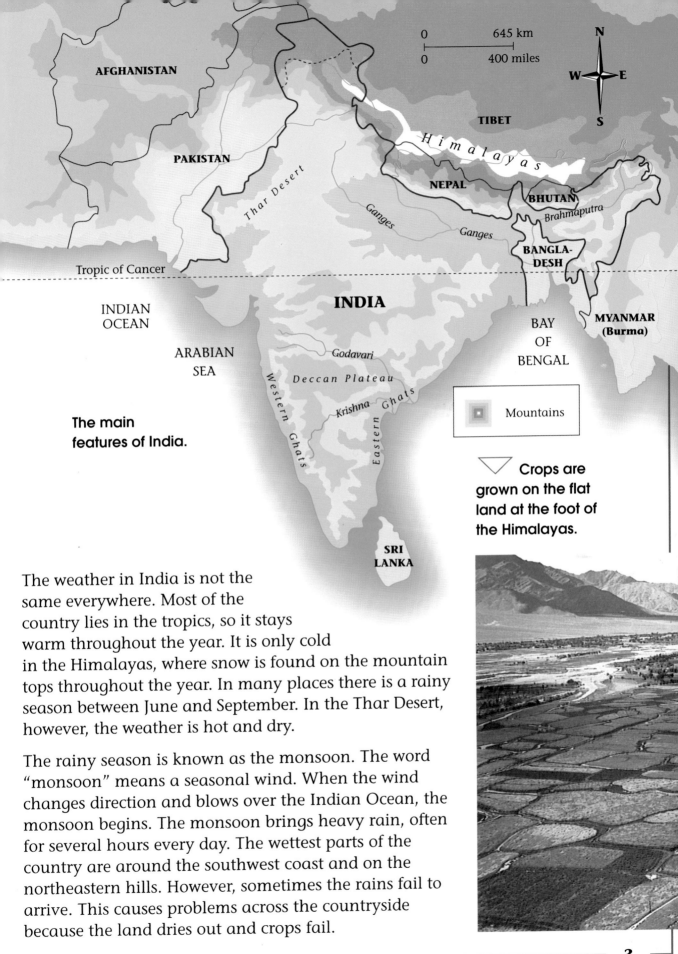

The main features of India.

Mountains

Crops are grown on the flat land at the foot of the Himalayas.

The weather in India is not the same everywhere. Most of the country lies in the tropics, so it stays warm throughout the year. It is only cold in the Himalayas, where snow is found on the mountain tops throughout the year. In many places there is a rainy season between June and September. In the Thar Desert, however, the weather is hot and dry.

The rainy season is known as the monsoon. The word "monsoon" means a seasonal wind. When the wind changes direction and blows over the Indian Ocean, the monsoon begins. The monsoon brings heavy rain, often for several hours every day. The wettest parts of the country are around the southwest coast and on the northeastern hills. However, sometimes the rains fail to arrive. This causes problems across the countryside because the land dries out and crops fail.

The People

In this large country, there are many contrasts in the way people live. There are many differences in the appearance, language, writing, customs, and religions of the Indian people.

There are eighteen official languages and hundreds of different dialects throughout India. Hindi is the most commonly used language, although only about one-fifth of the people speak it. English is the second language for many Indians. English or Hindi is often spoken when people from two different parts of the country meet. Many people speak or understand at least two languages. The Prime Minister in 1995, Narasimha Rao, speaks at least eight of the Indian languages.

Religion plays an important part in most people's lives in India. Eighty-three percent of Indian people belong to the **Hindu** faith. Hindus believe that after death, a person's soul is born again into another body. This rebirth is called reincarnation.

Every Hindu village in India has a temple, and most people belonging to this faith have a small shrine at home where they can pray. The **caste system** is a part of the Hindu religion. Lower caste people are generally poor. Traditionally, only very high caste Hindus, called Brahmins, can be priests. The very lowest castes were known as **untouchables**. The government in India has outlawed the idea of Untouchability.

Hindu festivals are celebrated throughout the year. The most well known is **Diwali**, the festival of light. Hindus often make a pilgrimage to the banks of the Ganges River, which they regard as a sacred river.

Although about 750 million Indians are Hindus, there are other important religions too. Just under 100 million people are **Muslims**, and about 49 million people are **Buddhists**, **Sikhs**, **Jains**, or Christians.

A Hindu wedding is a colorful and exciting event.

These Indian boys are being taught about their religion.

The Sikh, Jain, and Buddhist religions began in India. In the Sikh religion, only one God is worshiped, and there is no caste system. Buddhists follow the teachings of Buddha, who said that people are reincarnated until they reach a state of perfect peace, called nirvana. The Jain religion forbids people to hurt any living creature.

Indian culture, music, arts, and dances are often linked to religion. The best known musical instruments are the sitar (a stringed instrument) and the tabla (a twin drum). Dances may be based on religious stories. The dancers use complicated movements of the eyes, hands, and face to act out the story. Sports are also important. The Indian cricket team is one of the best in the world, and India has given the world the games of chess and polo.

Where Do People Live?

India has the second largest population in the world. In 1993 there were 903,000,000 people in India. The figure will probably rise to over one billion by the year 2000.

The Indian population is growing quickly because people generally have large families, particularly if they live in the country. In India, older people have to rely on their children to take care of them. If they have a large family they can be certain they will not be left alone in their old age. Also, until recently many infants died, but modern medicine has reduced the infant death rate. Now, many more children survive.

If you look at the map, you can see that most people live either on the flat lands of the north or around the coasts. The land is rich and fertile in these areas, and crops grow well. The **produce** feeds many people.

About three-quarters of all Indians live in the countryside. There are 650,000 villages in India. An average-sized village is home to about 1000 people. Most people who live in these villages work on the land, but some are craftspeople, doctors, teachers, or shopkeepers. Many farm workers have very small plots of land, and the food they grow feeds their families.

In the cities, modern buildings house the richer people, who may work in business or industry or as doctors, lawyers, or teachers. Office, factory, or shop workers often live in apartments built by the government. These people are not wealthy.

CITY
POPULATIONS
Millions (approx.)

City	Population
Bombay	12.5
Calcutta	11.0
Delhi	8.5
Madras	5.5
Bangalore	4.0
Ahmedabad	3.5
Poona	2.5
Kanpur	2.0
Nagpur	1.5
Lucknow	1.5
Jaipur	1.5

Mountains

Population
Dense
Medium
Sparse

△ **Where in India do people live?**

Poor people often live in makeshift housing. They find it difficult to get jobs, and when they do, they are often unskilled and poorly paid jobs, like building laborers, street cleaners, or servants.

There are advantages to living in a city. There are good schools, modern hospitals, and movie theaters, and there are more opportunities than in the country. But cities can be very crowded and polluted. There may be shortages of housing, clean water, and electricity because the cities are growing so fast.

◁ **Poor people in cities may live in houses like these, without electricity or running water.**

Indian cities will continue to grow as people migrate from the country. People believe life will be better in the city. However, it may not always turn out to be so.

Agriculture

Today India can grow enough food to feed its people. It is self-sufficient in food. In recent years, India has donated surplus grain (rice and wheat) to famine relief in Africa and other parts of Asia.

More than half of the people in India work in farming. Many farmers grow food to feed their own families, and their plots of land are small. If they have any food left over, they sell it at the local market. There are larger farms too, where food is mainly grown to sell for profit. About one-third of India's earnings from **exports** comes from the sale of agricultural produce.

There are also huge farms, called plantations, on which most of the crops are raised for export. Some, like cotton, may be processed by local factories. People who work on a plantation usually live there, too. They live in houses provided by the plantation owner. Children go to the plantation school, and there probably are a shop and a medical center, too. Tea, cotton, spices, jute, tobacco, coffee, and sugar are typical plantation crops grown in India.

India's farmers face many problems. Many people have to rent land, and the plots are usually very small. If the crops fail, the farmers cannot pay their rent, and they get into debt. Sometimes the monsoon rains fail, bringing drought and a poor harvest. The people have struggled to improve their farming methods. Money from the government and aid from overseas groups like Oxfam have helped. Many areas now have better seeds and **irrigation** systems. It is mainly the richer landowners with large farms who have been helped by these new farming methods. Many of the poorer farmers, especially those who have gotten into debt, have had to move to the cities because they cannot make a decent living in the country. When they leave the land, it is taken back by the landlords—so the rich farmers get even richer.

▷ Irrigation systems channel the water to where it is needed.

△ **Paddy fields are flooded with water so that the rice plants will grow.**

Rice is the main food crop for most Indians. Wheat is grown in the cooler northern areas, and millet is grown all over India. Rice farmers need plenty of water during the growing season, because rice plants will not grow unless they are standing in water. Oxfam has helped some villages to build little dams called check dams. These stop rainwater from flowing away and help to build up underground water supplies. These supplies can then be used for crops and drinking water.

Reliable water supplies have helped, but so have the scientific advances of the **Green Revolution**. India's farmers now produce three times as much grain as they did in 1947. More crops are grown on each farm. However, the Green Revolution has brought problems. Chemicals used to fertilize the crops and to kill weeds and pests can seep into the rivers. Water may become polluted and can poison the environment. The Green Revolution has really only worked for the larger farmers, who have the money to afford the new seeds and chemicals.

Industry

India is one of the most important industrial countries in the world. Many workers are highly skilled, and the modern education system trains many young people to work in industry. India produces everything from chemicals and cars to computers. Huge power stations generate electricity. All towns and most villages have electricity.

Upon independence in 1947, the Indian government realized that the country needed strong industry in order to develop and become wealthy. Money was invested (spent) to help industries grow.

One of the most important and successful industrial areas is the Damodar Valley west of Calcutta. Other big industrial areas have grown around large cities like Bombay and Madras.

Big industrial areas face problems. Waste from factories can cause severe water and air pollution that make areas unsafe to live in. The wealth that industries create is limited. Also, when modern machinery is used to do the work, fewer jobs are created for people. Only those people living close to the factories are likely to benefit from them. The government has decided to spend money to help industry grow in the countryside. Small-scale projects and factories employing many people have been set up. These workers use simple machines and tools, but use their own skills much more.

The hand-loom industry is an example. Cloth-making is a good industry because it employs many people. India grows the cotton, and many people already have the skills needed to do this kind of work.

▽ **This man and boy are weaving cloth in a small factory.**

Indian clothes are fashionable all over the world. A lot of India's colorful cotton fabric is sold abroad. It is much better for countries such as India, which produce raw materials, to export finished goods, such as cloth and clothing. Other countries will pay more for finished goods than for raw materials.

In the past, many poorer countries suffered from unfair trade. They sold their raw materials at low prices to other countries, such as the United Kingdom. Those countries turned them into finished goods. They could then charge higher prices for these goods and earn much more money. In the end, these manufacturing countries made more money than the people of India, who grew the raw materials in the first place. Such trading still goes on today.

Industrialization has brought a higher standard of living to many Indians. However, the benefits must be weighed against the costs. Some workers are exploited (taken advantage of) by both foreign and Indian companies, which pay lower wages than they would in the United States or United Kindom. Safety standards are often poor. In 1984, people living in the city of Bhopal suffered from poisonous gases that escaped from an American-owned chemical factory. Thousands of people were killed and thousands more injured—many permanently.

△ Industry is important in India, but the pollution it creates is a problem.

Staying Healthy

Poor health is linked to poverty. But what is poverty? It is being too poor to have enough to eat, and it can also mean being homeless. In 1972, the **United Nations** said that about half of India's population was living in poverty. Now only 25 percent of people are classed as being very poor by the United Nations. Many **development agencies** say that the real figure is closer to 40 percent, or about 360 million people.

How long people can expect to live is linked to their health, and people's health can be affected by poverty. India has improved the standard of health for many people in recent years. If you were born in India in 1960, you could expect to live only about 44 years. Now, most people live into their sixties.

A clean water supply is very important for good health. Many diseases are transmitted (passed on) through water. It is not hard to understand how epidemics can occur. For example, people may take their water from a river into which sewage drains. If they use water that is infected by the bacteria that cause cholera, for example, they can become sick very quickly and may die. Typhoid and dysentery are also diseases which can be transmitted through water. The symptoms of each are different, but all cause fever, sickness, and diarrhea. Malaria, which is carried by mosquitoes, is also linked with water. Mosquitoes live in wet, swampy places. Malaria can cause fever and illness for many years.

▽ **People like this boy can be treated quickly when accidents happen.**

The Indian government knows how important it is to have a clean and safe water supply. Wells have been built in most villages to provide people with safe water. Now nearly 90 percent of the population lives in a place with a clean water supply. Only 50 percent had a clean water supply in the 1970s.

The people most at risk from illness and disease are young children. In poor countries, many babies die from diseases like typhoid and polio before their first birthday. Children need a balanced diet to be strong and healthy. They also need to be protected against serious infections, like tuberculosis and polio. The number of **infant deaths** in India has been cut in half over the last 30 years.

There are medical centers in most villages. Traveling clinics reach the most remote places. Most children are now vaccinated against serious diseases: 96 percent against tuberculosis and 89 percent against diphtheria and polio.

Unfortunately, babies are still dying—mainly those born to the poorest families. Poor families may not be able to give their children a balanced diet. The children are not starving, but they are most likely to be seriously ill with measles or diarrhea. These diseases will not kill well-fed babies, but will kill those that are weak already. The health of India's population has greatly improved, but there is still a long way to go. Health services enjoyed by the richest Indians need to be brought to the poorest in the country, too.

These villagers are getting water from a well built with funds from the charity Oxfam.

The Village of Raipole

Raipole is a large village, almost like a small town, in the state of Andhra Pradesh, which is in the south of India. The maps show the location of the state and also of the village of Raipole itself.

Andhra Pradesh is a little larger than Colorado. In 1991 there were 66 million people living there, compared to 3.3 million in Colorado. On the flat land around the coast, the weather is hot all year, with plenty of rain. Inland on the **plateau**, the weather is very dry for about six months (November to April). The monsoon brings the rains, which usually begin in May.

Raipole is on the higher plateau land, inland from the coast. The village is home to about 2,000 people. This is larger than average for an Indian village.

Most people in Raipole farm the surrounding land. Rice is the main food crop, but vegetables and spices are also grown.

▽ **The marketplace in Raipole is colorful and crowded.**

▷ **These women are collecting water from an outdoor faucet shared by the villagers in Raipole.**

Village life is very busy. In the village, there are several shops, two schools, and a marketplace. There are also two places of worship, one for Hindus and one for Muslims.

Raipole is connected by road to the nearest town, Ibrahimpatan. For most people, life is centered in the village. They are born, grow up, and marry there. They bring up their own families in the village, too.

▽ **Andhra Pradesh and the village of Raipole.**

INDIA

ANDHRA PRADESH

N
W E
S

0   100   200km

MAHARASHTRA

ORISSA

MADHYA PRADESH

Vizianagaram

Anakapalle • Visakhapatnam

Nizamabad

Godavari River

Warangal

Rajahmundry

Secunderabad

Ibrahimpatan

Hyderabad   River

Krishna   Eluru

Mahbubnagar   Vijayawada

Guntur

Tenali

Nagarjunasagar Dam

Bay of Bengal

Kurnool • Ongole

ANDHRA PRADESH

Adoni

Guntakal • Gooty

Nellore

Cuddapah

Tirupathi

Madras

KARNATAKA   Chittoor

Bangalore •

TAMIL NADU

RAIPOLE VILLAGE

ZPPH School

Post Office

Health Clinic

Water Tank

Kanaka Durga Temple

Rice Mill

Muslim Mazid

Primary School

15

Village Life

In Raipole most of the villagers work on the land. Some own their own land; others work as day-laborers for landlords. Rice is the main crop. It is often sold for profit, but is also grown to feed the villagers. Rice is grown on irrigated land. Water collected during the rainy season is stored in irrigation ponds, called tanks, and then channeled to the **paddy fields** when needed. There is a rice mill in the village. This is a small factory where the husks, or coverings, are removed from the grains to make the rice ready to sell at the market.

△ The wool from the sheep is spun into thread, ready to be sold.

About 50 families in the village are shepherds. Each family keeps about 200 sheep. The sheep graze on the land surrounding the paddy fields. Shepherds make a living by selling both the wool and the lambs.

Not everyone in the village is a farmer or shepherd. There are shopkeepers, a blacksmith (who makes and mends tools), cobblers (who make shoes and sandals and other leather goods), a vet, a doctor, and several teachers. Fourteen families work as potters, making roof tiles as well as pots. There are also weavers. They make the beautiful silks used to make saris, the traditional dress of Hindu women.

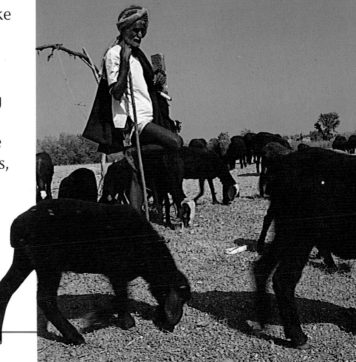

▷ A shepherd takes his flock of sheep to graze in the countryside.

A job you may not have heard of is that of the **toddy tapper**. Toddy is a very popular drink made from the juice collected (or tapped) from palm trees. More than 50 families make their living tapping toddy in Raipole.

The carpenters in the village make and mend anything from doors to plows to babies' cots. Washerwomen make a living by doing other people's laundry. There is also a baker. Religious leaders live and work in Raipole. The village has both a Muslim Imam and a Hindu priest.

Most of the village children attend school. But they are also expected to do some of the family's work. They often help after school and during vacations, earning much needed money for their families.

△ These women are selling their goods at the market in Raipole.

School

△ Children arriving at the ZPPH School in Raipole.

In India, all children between the ages of five and fourteen can go to school. In fact, not everyone attends regularly. Children are sometimes needed to help their parents in their work. The government has made "Education for All" one of its most important aims. In Andhra Pradesh, only 56 percent of men and 34 percent of women can read and write. This figure will improve as the present generation of children grows up. Many children today go to school, while their parents did not.

In Raipole there is a place at school for everyone. The two schools in the village are the Zilla Praja Parishad High School (ZPPH School) and a privately owned primary school.

Most children attend the ZPPH School. The school has 750 students in 10 classes. Children start here when they are five, and most leave when they are fourteen. You will notice from the pictures that all the children dress in uniforms.

School starts at 10:00 A.M. with an outdoor assembly. A boy or girl reads the headlines from the newspaper to all the children. Next the children sing the national anthem before going to the classroom. The children study math, social studies, general science, Hindi, and English. Telugu, the local language, is also taught. Children learn about modern farming methods and health and hygiene.

Although religion is very important to Indian culture, India is a **secular** state. This means that children do not study religious education in school.

The students have an hour off after classes finish at 1:00 P.M. They all bring a lunch from home. The boys usually take theirs into the field and play. The girls get together at a friend's house. After lunch, everyone goes back to school until 4:00 P.M. In the afternoon, the boys and girls are put into separate groups to play sports and games. When they get home, they help their families either in the home or with their work.

These children are studying their textbooks during a history lesson.

Spare Time

People in India work very hard. Their day is long. Many adults, especially women, start work soon after dawn and only finish at dusk. People take a long lunch break in the middle of the day because it is very hot. People do manage to find some free time. They relax and spend their time in many different ways.

Raipole is in the country, and people have different opportunities than those living in the towns and cities. In the towns there are movie theaters and restaurants. Cricket matches take place, and there is always something to see and do.

The villagers of Raipole also enjoy their spare time, but in different ways. The children often play cricket after school. Adults, mainly the men, meet in the evenings, after the day's work is done. In Raipole there is a tree in the marketplace with a cement platform built around it. This is a very popular meeting place, where the men gather to discuss the news or to talk about village life. The tea stand is another busy meeting place where people can chat over a drink.

These children do not have stumps for the wicket, but they still enjoy a game of cricket.

Movies are probably the most popular form of entertainment in India. More films are made every year in India than in any other country. The villagers of Raipole have to catch a bus to the nearest town to visit the movie theater. Many people enjoy watching films on television, although most families do not have a television set. Groups of neighbors sometimes gather at a friend's house to watch their favorite programs.

Family and friends gather around the television to watch a film.

Religion is an important part of everyone's life. Most people are Hindu and regularly visit the temple in the village. In many homes there is an altar at which the family can pray. There is also a mosque for the Muslim people in Raipole. Religious festivals are often celebrated, and a wedding is a big village occasion. Most people in the village attend, and a huge feast is prepared to celebrate the occasion.

Veerachari's Day

Veerachari is ten years old, and he lives with his family in Raipole. In India families are often large, and it is common for grandparents, aunts, uncles, and cousins to live together. Veerachari has two sisters and a baby brother. His grandfather and his cousin also live with the family. This is a small family by Indian standards.

The house in which Veerachari lives has five rooms. Three rooms are bedrooms, one room is a living room, and the other room is the carpentry workshop. There is no bathroom or kitchen. Water has to be collected every day from an outdoor faucet shared by many people. The family washes and cooks outside the house in the yard. The yard is as much a part of the home as the bedrooms or living room.

△ Because Veerachari wants to become a doctor, he must study hard at school.

Veerachari goes to the ZPPH school. He is in the sixth grade, and Telugu (the local language) is his favorite subject. He bicycles to school every day and gives his cousin a ride.

After school, Veerachari cycles home and changes out of his uniform. He is expected to help his father in the carpentry workshop when he gets home.

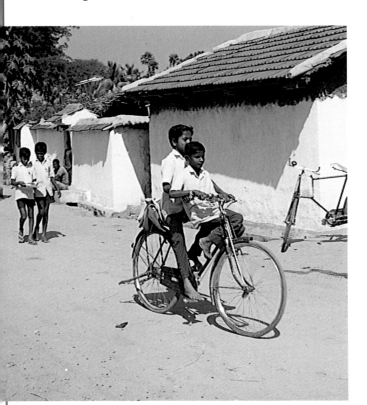

◁ Veerachari gives his cousin a ride to school on the crossbar of his bicycle.

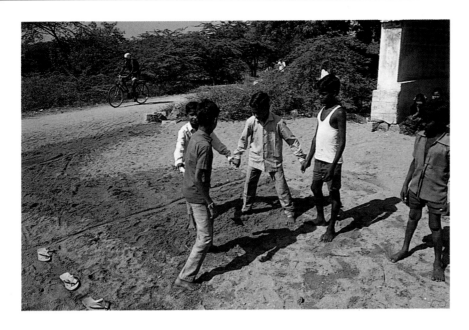

Boys enjoy a game of kabbadi after a hard day's work.

Neither of his parents went to school, but his father is a skilled carpenter. He learned his skill from his father, as most people of his generation did. When Veerachari leaves school, he does not want to become a carpenter. Instead, he hopes to go to a university to learn to be a doctor.

Veerachari usually has time to play with his friends in the village before his evening meal and bedtime. His favorite game is kabbadi. This is a kind of tag. There are two teams. One team tries to run from one side of the field to the other. The second team has to stop them.

As soon as he gets home from school, Veerachari helps his father with the carpentry.

Traveling Around Raipole

In Andhra Pradesh, transportation networks are not so well developed as in some other parts of the country. Only about 43 percent of all the villages are connected by all-weather paved roads. There are only about eighteen cars for every thousand people in the state. Bicycles and carts are far more common.

The pictures of the village show that the roads in and around Raipole are just dirt tracks. These are fine for most of the year, but it is very difficult to use motor vehicles on them during the rainy season, when the tracks turn to mud.

Most people travel on foot during the day. The distances to work and school are no more than about 1.25 miles. No one commutes to town every day. Most families own a bicycle, and short distances can be traveled quickly.

▽ **Villagers squeeze aboard a truck ready to set off for a wedding.**

Heavy loads like harvested rice or castor seeds are carried from the fields to market in a cart pulled by oxen.

For the people of Raipole, the bus is the main method of transportation for longer distances. The village does not have a railroad nearby. The bus stop is in the center of the village, and buses run regularly all day to Ibrahimpatan. Buses are cheap to use and are owned by the government.

A less common type of transportation is a tractor or truck. These are useful when a large group wants to travel together. For example, the photograph opposite shows villagers on a truck. They are all going to a wedding in the next village. Tractors and trucks are rented, and as many people as possible squeeze on to share the cost.

Journeys

Although about three-quarters of India's population lives in the countryside, 232,500,000 people live in the towns and cities (almost the same number of people as the entire population of the United States). By the year 2000, there will probably be more than 300 million living in the cities and towns.

Every year, many people leave the country to live in the nearest town or city. They must journey across the country by bus, rail, or even air. Townspeople also travel to visit their relatives in their home villages.

Some people may **emigrate** to places like Canada or the Persian Gulf States. In the 1960s many Indians went to live in the United Kingdom, too. To visit relatives abroad, Indians may choose to travel by air. *Air India* is the Indian airline company that flies to most of the world's largest countries. *Indian Airlines* operates within the country. However, travel by air is expensive, and only richer people can afford the fares.

▽ **This man is running to catch his bus as it arrives in a small town.**

India is famous for its railroads. It has the fourth largest rail network in the world. There are more than 37,000 miles of track. Every day 11 million passengers travel by train. Most of the older railroad lines were built by the British in the 19th century. Since then, India has updated some of its lines and introduced diesel and electric trains in places. But you may still see steam locomotives working today, and some tourists come specially to India to "train spot." Locomotives driven by steam are used because there is plenty of coal in India to fuel them.

△ Travelers arrive and prepare to leave at New Delhi railroad station.

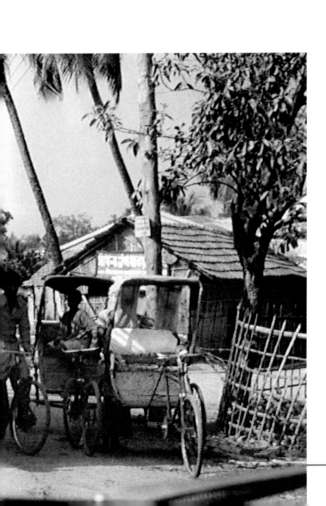

People who leave the country to live in the towns usually travel by train. Most small towns and large villages are connected to the rail network. Passengers can carry most of their belongings on trains.

Bus and railroad routes are closely linked. All railroad stations are on a bus route, and people can go anywhere by bus. India's main roads are fairly good, and it is sometimes quicker to travel by bus than by train. Many of the buses are comfortable, and some have videos. Only the richest people have their own cars in India. There are about two cars for every thousand people in India compared to about four hundred for every thousand people in wealthier countries.

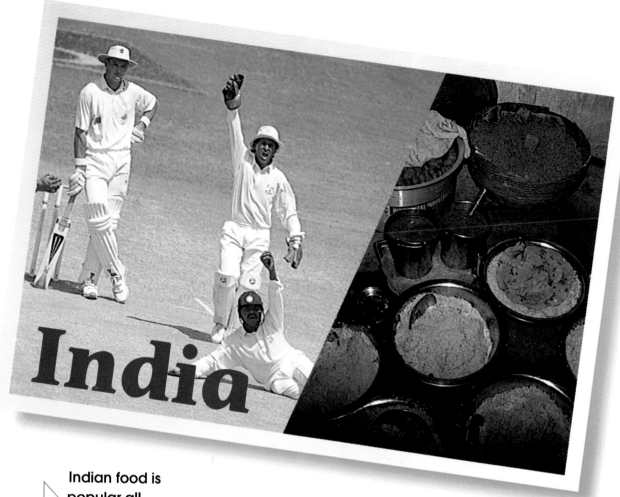

India

▷ Indian food is popular all over the world.

△ India's cricket teams in action.

India today is a mixture of old and new, with both ancient and modern ways of life. Many of the people's lives and living standards are similar to those in Western countries. But of course, there are many poor people, too.

We have many images of a country in our minds, even if we have never actually visited the place. One of the main aims of this book is to encourage you to realize that India is a huge and varied country. Although there is great poverty in India, there is also great richness of culture. The photographs in this book show some of these aspects of India.

India is a country with many natural riches. Its landscape is beautiful. There are useful natural resources to be found in the rocks and the soil. And there are many famous temples and monuments, like the Taj Mahal.

The people of India have faced many struggles since 1947, when the country became independent from British rule. The ever-growing population has needed more food, more jobs, and more housing, year after year. Foreign countries have helped by giving loans, grants, and advice to help the country develop. Charities like Oxfam have also given their assistance. However, the people of India themselves have improved their own lives by sheer hard work and determination. By reading this book you will have gained an insight into the lives of Indian people today.

▽ The Taj Mahal.

▷ A colorful display of saris in a market.

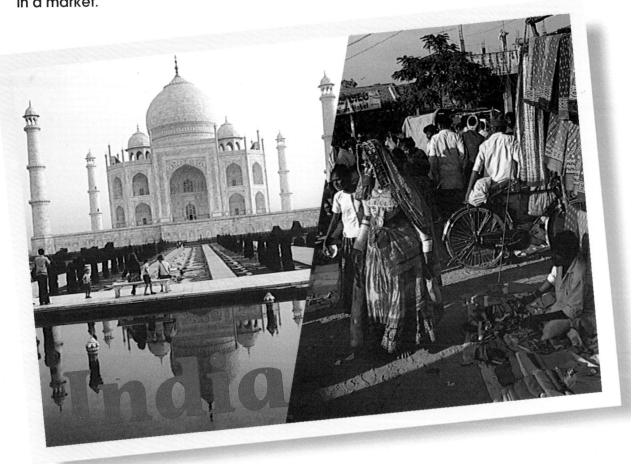

Glossary

Buddhism This religion began in India in 500 B.C. and has spread all over the world. Buddhists teach that people die and are reborn many times, but that they can eventually reach a state of perfect peace called nirvana.

Caste System A type of class system linked to the Hindu religion. Caste is decided by birth and cannot be changed. People born into a high caste can have the best jobs, while the lower castes get the dirtiest and most poorly paid jobs.

Democracy A democratic country has a government which has been freely elected by the people. Adults vote at an election for the government of their choice.

Development agency A group or organization set up to improve living conditions for people living in poorer countries. Sometimes charities fund such groups, and governments may also contribute money to pay for Development Agencies.

Diwali A festival of the Hindu year, celebrated in either October or November. It is known as the festival of light.

Emigration The permanent movement of people from one country to another.

Export Goods that are sold to or traded with another country.

Gandhi, Mahatma A famous Indian who devoted himself to achieving independence for India from the British in the 1940s. He led the people in a movement of non-violent protest.

Green Revolution Scientific advances made in farming beginning in the 1960s. Fast-growing seeds and chemicals were developed which greatly increased crop production.

Hinduism This is one of the oldest religions in the world, dating to before 1000 B.C. Hinduism has many gods. Hindus believe in rebirth or reincarnation.

Infant deaths A term used to describe the number of babies who die in the first year of life.

Irrigation This is a way of providing water for plants by using channels or pipes.

Jain(ism) The Jain religion has many similarities to Buddhism. It was founded in the 6th century by Mahvira. Many Jains live in south and southwest India. They are strict vegetarians and avoid injury to all living things.

Muslim Muslims follow the Islamic religion, which was founded by the prophet Mohammed in the 7th century. His teachings are written in their holy book, the Qu'an.

Paddy field A small rice field with raised banks, called bunds around the outsides. When heavy rains fall, the bunds trap the water inside the field so that it is flooded. Rice begins to grow in the flooded field.

Plateau An area of highland with a flat top.

Produce Crops grown or animals raised by farming.

Secular Not religious. A secular state is one whose government does not base its laws on religion.

Sikh The Sikh religion was founded in the 15th century. Sikhs live in the state of Punjab. The religion is similar to Hinduism, but there is no caste system.

Toddy Tapper A person who collects the juice from the toddy tree.

United Nations (UN) An international organization founded after World War II to promote and maintain peace and to help poor countries to become wealthier.

Untouchables Under the caste system, untouchables are members of the lowest group of Hindus. Traditionally the dirtiest jobs are reserved for untouchables. Recently the Indian Government has made it illegal to discriminate against these people.

Index

About Oxfam in India

Oxfam America works in partnership with communities in Asia, Africa, the Americas, and the Caribbean to find long term solutions to poverty and hunger. Oxfam America supports the self-help efforts of poor people—especially women, landless farm workers, and survivors of war and natural disasters—who are working to make their lives better. Oxfam America believes that all people have the basic rights to earn a living and to have food, shelter, health care, and education.

Oxfam America is part of the international family of Oxfam organizations that work in more than 70 countries. In India, Oxfam concentrates on helping poor communities come together to help them have more control over their lives and obtain resources to which they are entitled. As well as providing funds, Oxfam gives advice and training to local groups. Particular attention is given to the problems that women face in India. Oxfam is also dealing with environmental problems, such as the effects of drought and the loss of forest land.

© 1996 Rigby Education
Published by Rigby Interactive Library,
an imprint of Rigby Education,
division of Reed Elsevier, Inc.
500 Coventry Lane
Crystal Lake, IL 60014

Printed in Hong Kong
Designed and produced by Visual Image
Cover design by Threefold Design

00 99 98 97 96
10 9 8 7 6 5 4 3 2 1

Library of Congress Cataloging-in-Publication Data

Barker, Amanda, 1959-
    India / Amanda Barker,
        p.   cm. -- (Worldfocus)
    Includes index.
    Summary: Introduces India through a geographical and historical profile and case studies of individuals and of a representative community.
    ISBN 1-57572-028-0 (lib. bdg.)
    1. India--Juvenile literature. [1. India.] I.
Title. II. Series.
DS407.B347 1996
954--dc20   95-25031

Acknowledgments

The author and publishers would like to thank the following for their help with this book: Oxfam (UK and Ireland): Joe Human and Lorraine Collett from the Asia Desk; the staff of the photo library; and the Education workers who commented on early drafts; Sam Kenrick and the Oxfam Hederabad office for help in organizing photography; the photographer, R. Lokanadham, of the Centre for Development Communication, Hyderabad; and the people of Raipole.

The author and publishers wish to acknowledge, with thanks, the following photographic sources:

Oxfam p. 29/Oxfam T. Parker pp. 2, 26; B. Buxton p. 3; M. Wells pp. 5, 12; J. Ogle pp. 6, 10, 11; T. Stack p. 9; J. Wild p. 9; S. Safa p. 13; Centre for Development Communication, Hyderabad/R. Lokanadham pp. 4, 14, 15, 16, 17, 18, 19, 20, 21, 22, 23, 24, 25, 28r, 29r, Peter Sanders p. 27; Ben Radford/Allsport p. 28l.

Every effort has been made to contact copyright holders of material published in this book. Any omissions will be rectified in subsequent printings if notice is given to the publisher.

Cover photograph: © Oxfam/Tricia Parker—father and child in a village in Rajasthan